VICTUS

The Andrew D. Scott Story

Building an Appetite to Take on the World!

Colleagues that have inspired me thus far on the journey:

- Chris Wayne-Wills - CEO Macdonald Hotels
- Jillian Maclean - Drake & Morgan
- David Cochrane - HiT Scotland
- Gordon McIntyre - City of Glasgow College
- Hitesh Patel - Paperchase Accountancy
- Kevin Timoney - Pelican Procurement Services
- David Sands – Businessman & Entrepreneur
- Jillian Sheddon – Knockhill Racing Circuit

VICTUS

Building an Appetite to Take on the World!

VICTUS

Noun:

Living, a way of life, nourishment, provision, diet, that which sustains life.

Andrew D. Scott & Michael Patterson

www.victusconsultancy.co.uk
www.michaeldavidpatterson.com

VICTUS

Copyright © 2015 Andrew D. Scott and Michael Patterson

All Worldwide Rights Reserved

All rights reserved.

No part of this publication may be reproduced, stored in a retrieval system, or transmitted in any form, or by any means, electronic, mechanical, recorded, photocopied, or otherwise, without the prior permission of the copyright holder, except by a reviewer, who may quote brief passages in a review.

ISBN: 978-1-326-11185-4

Dedicated to my father

David Nicol Scott

A man who taught me many great things, none more so than:

"The time to break a twig is when you see it."

To address issues, face up to challenges and deal with things there and then with energy, vitality and vigour.

Thank you Dad x

VICTUS

"The things my father said would make me a better man."

Black Stone Cherry

"The sole purpose of this book is to make us better, for change to occur. If no change, then there is no point. Ask yourself how you will be changed by this work and more importantly, what is the change you seek?

The 'recipes' shared herein, give people a flavour, feel and taste of what Victus can do for them. We want to make our potential clients think and begin a process........one that leads to Action!"

Andrew D. Scott MiH
Victus Consultancy

VICTUS

FOREWORD

Congratulations....... You've taken the first step, clearly you have a desire to improve things, a need to seek something better, to raise the bar on your achievements and perhaps learn from others. This book is a highly thought provoking, interesting read.

I'm privileged to have known Andrew for nearly 20 years and to have witnessed the growth of him as an individual and of his companies

As a consistent high achiever Andrew has recognised the need to surround himself with great people and the need to focus on quality and consistency in his businesses. This book will provide you with a humorous romp through stories, anecdotes and lessons learned.

It's never orthodox, from the safety and comfort of the corporate environment that has been my career, sometimes it can look scary but I'm never underwhelmed by what he and his teams have achieved.

Andrew and his team have always delivered. They follow through on promises and genuinely never let a client down.
If you're tempted to engage the services of VICTUS Consultancy then this book will give you a taste of what you can expect. Ronald Reagan famously said, "Hope is not a plan" however never give up on hope because hope is driven from your faith and belief in what you're doing.

The faith you had when you started is still there and I would be confident that perhaps the best thing that Andrew and the VICTUS team can give you is to remind you that you're on the right course.

Think of them as the Sat Nav directing you to achieving greater things.
I hope you enjoy the book and wish you every success in improving your business.

Chris Wayne Wills
(CEO) MACDONALD HIGHLAND RESORT

Building an Appetite to Take on the World!

Contents

Marmalade and Duffle Coats 13

The Adrian Mole Years 16

Caffe Latte 19

In the Slipstream 20

The Perfect Appetizer 25

Creating a Chocolate Heaven 30

Pizza, Passion and Cherries 32

Delivering a Surprise Performance 35

Statue of Liberty 38

Polka Dot, It Suits You 43

Ask the Question 46

Knightsbridge & Kevin Bridges 49

In Bed with Timeless 55

A Genuine Dish Worth Sharing 56

Get Your 5 a Day 57

Gibraltar Kev 60

Becoming Einstein 62

Employ a Goalkeeper 64

Best Before	66
The Winner Is	67
Shaken Not Stirred	71
Happy New Year	75
Once Upon a Time	80
Ssshh	81
Inside the Kitchen	87
Become a Master of Cheese	90
Dollars, Euros, Ideas & Pounds	94
Under Starters Orders	95

Marmalade and Duffle Coats

Be warned, I speak at speed!
My... text... is... not... to... be... read... at... a ...slow... calm... considered... rate.

I speak quickly, with an upbeat tempo, it's a rapid read. Like a modern day auctioneer competing in the public speaking arena. Quick off the mark, thrusting forward with a competitive edge. My remarks aim to be positive, fast paced, stimulating and thought provoking.

For those of you who know me, you can visualize my animated actions, my flailing arms, my facial expressions and mannerisms. You can hear my voice, it's tone and intonation. For those that don't, I look forward to meeting up and working with you in the coming weeks and months ahead.

I was born Andrew David Scott on the 25th of June 1974 in Glasgow. I share my birth date with a remarkable individual from Peru.....Paddington Bear. This may explain my love of marmalade and a rather large duffle coat on the back seat of my Mercedes!

With the exception of a brief stop in Fife from age five to eight, I was raised in three residential areas on the outskirts of the disputed Second City of the Empire.

As I arrived in each new property in Rutherglen, Clarkston and Newton Mearns, I unknowingly became more elegant, eloquent, refined and educated. You simply cannot say, "Newton Mearns," without sounding intelligent!

At 18 I attended Glasgow College of Food Technology, working weekends at an established hotel in Pitlochry. After my culinary studies, I was successful in landing a role at the impressive Green Hotel in Perthshire, working 60 hours per week learning the trade.

Then a stint beckoned at the Jarvis Caledonia in Ayr. It was here that in the short space of four months, I transformed their loss making bars into major money making operations, a real cash bonanza. I had spotted many shortcomings and failings within days of starting and like my wise father said, "the time to break a twig is when you see it!" So, I duly obliged. I addressed the issues and plugged the aforementioned gaps. Continuing on my learning curve, I was appointed General Manager at the luxurious Inverbeg Inn at the tender age of twenty-two.

The last decade has seen me develop the Scott Hospitality Services Group including the Heaven Scent Coffee Shops, and oversee hospitality concessions at race tracks and other Corporate venues. Operating bespoke catering services for weddings, functions and gatherings, both at home and abroad. I received more recognition and praise when in 2012 I won the HiT Entrepreneurial Caterer of the Year, followed in 2014 by the Hospitality Industry Trust Frank Mullen scholarship.

As Victus is fast becoming established as an innovative, productive and rewarding consultancy firm to work with within the industry, it seems only natural to add keynote speaking, books and training seminars alongside TV and radio expertise on the menu.

The Adrian Mole Years

When I became a teenager I stepped into a place that I had never been before, I ventured into the unknown. I had worked previously delivering newspapers and as a door to door bacon boy, but this was a proper job, working with other people, older people..........grown-ups!

These adults however, were not normal, they were a breed apart. They were complicated, clever, mystical vagabonds and creators, they were chefs!

I had stepped into the kitchen of Parklands Country Club in Newton Mearns. Something happened back then, there was a noise, a smell, a heat that has been with me to this very day. They spoke a language that was foreign.

This wasn't any old kitchen but a fully operational seven corner commercial kitchen. There was a sauce corner, a sweet corner, a veg and soup station. There were ovens and grills, brat pans and salamanders, stock pots,

walk in fridges, blast chillers and machines that to this day
I'm still not sure what they do!

All I know is............ I was hooked!

As I said, I was 13. People my age were playing football, chatting up girls, buying the latest CDs, but not me. I was immersed in stocks, sauces and syrups, learning about reductions and sur la plate vegetables. I learned knife skills, hygiene awareness, stock rotation knowledge and I thought that I could cook!

I had been part time cheffing for about two months when I offered constructive criticism to my mum's evening meal on one particular night.

Holy Moly!

I was met with, "The day you can cook like Ramsay is the day you can talk like Ramsay." Needless to say, we shall just put that episode down to a school boy error.

In the intervening years, I became aware that there is surprisingly little difference between a candidate with six months of experience and one with six years. The real difference comes from the individual's dedication, personality and intelligence. 'Newton Mearns.'

While you're busy navigating your day today, think about what you couldn't live without, the stuff that makes your life that little bit easier.

All those things you didn't even realise you needed until someone brought them to market.

Every product or service ever created was born from a problem that needed to be solved, or a desire that was waiting to be fulfilled.

Those *Innocent* smoothie boys say that if you can't sell your pitch to your granny in 30 seconds, then you don't have a business. Get counting .....

Victus can help new starts flourish, existing fourth generation businesses that have lost their way, or companies looking to expand their present offering.

Advice, guidance, hands on mentoring, every client needs a different level of assistance and support.
Why Victus? Because we currently own and operate many successful businesses within the hospitality industry. We are relevant, we move with the times, we listen and we enable YOU to build and develop long term strategies and solutions.

Settle down to read with a little cappuccino and we'll begin................

Caffe Latte

Like several of my favourite recipe books, 'Victus' is an invaluable resource.

You don't have to start on page one and work your way through. Each principle or formula stands on its own. Reawaken a thought or an idea you've already had. Spark new ones. Discover different ways of thinking about what you do and how you tell your story.

It is a vital pocket book that you can 'dip' in and out of! One that you can return to regularly, that you'll find beneficial and can relate to. Satisfying, rewarding and highly addictive. That little expresso to get you 'started' at the beginning of each day.

✘ *Now, go make your idea count!*

In the Slipstream

After my own preferred hot drink in the morning, I love to cycle. Pedaling the streets, paths and countryside throughout the historic Kingdom of Fife.

As well as obvious health and fitness benefits, I recognise I also make many of my most inspired business decisions whilst out on the road. I find numerous questions and answers arrive in 'tandem' in equal measure.

One that came to mind on a recent journey was:
How on earth did UK cycling go from the depths of despair in 1996 to world domination in 2012? From being a laughing stock to becoming an organisation and team worthy of high level approaches from arch rivals? Strange what the mind conjures up cycling to Tesco and back.

The multitude of thoughts racing through my mind in response, included –

The best opportunity to remodel your business is when you are at rock bottom with your back to the wall – you must make big decisions, make them quickly and implement them energetically with a confidence that will enable you to fend off criticism.
Always employ the very best people you can get and give them all the support and funding they need. Let them take the credit for success – but stand beside them if there are setbacks.

Create and maintain a team ethos across your staff and with your board. At all times do, and be, the best that you possibly can be –

and encourage and inspire everyone in your team to do the same.
Make sure your business is professionally driven and not amateur led. Build on your strengths, but also work hard on your weaknesses.

Pay attention to every detail, however small or seemingly insignificant. You too can aggregate those marginal gains to achieve success in your business.

When you set yourselves targets, set them high. Think the unthinkable. Aim for the stars and who knows what might happen."
Now, all of the aforementioned is good, solid, sensible advice and counsel. Ten times more than required though. A more concise cycling analogy may be this:

*In July 2014 a rider overtook me on a local cycle path. For the next ten minutes, I rode right behind him, drafting in his progress, sitting in his slipstream. Sure, there's an aerodynamic reason that this works, but the real reason is mental, not based on physics. It works because, right in front of me is proof............***that I can go faster!***

Without knowing it, we do this at work every day. We set our pace based on what competitors or co-workers are doing. One secret to making more of an impact then, is figuring out who you intend to follow. Don't 'pace yourself.' Instead, find someone to unknowingly pace you.

Maybe no one knows who you are right now, and that's fine. Being obscure can be a great position to be in. Be happy you're in the shadows, the slipstream. Use this time to make mistakes without the whole world hearing about them. Keep fine tuning. Work out the kinks. Test random ideas. Try new things. No one knows you, so it's no big deal if you mess up. Obscurity helps protect your ego and preserve your confidence. Now's the time to take risks without worrying about embarrassing yourself.

I personally, ride in the slipstream of Jillian Maclean, founder of Drake & Morgan, a London based bar group. From its inception in 2008 Jillian has been the nerve centre. Her creative mind and sheer genius brought together contemporary, fresh and original ideas from all around the world to help her

daring venture thrive and succeed. Like UK cycling she received approaches from high level admirers waiting in the wings.
Whilst building her impressive portfolio of restaurants, she was in high demand. Tatler magazine, Harrods, Fortnum & Mason all wanted her to do pop up shops, give presentations or go to conferences to be a keynote speaker, they flew her around the world to be with the best of the best.

From meeting with Jillian on several occasions, a quote of hers I enjoy is "Come on in, the water is lovely." Basically inviting any like-minded individuals to come and try it, stick a toe in the water and see how you feel about it. My thoughts in addition to that would be, "It is lovely, however sometimes seeking the idyllic lakeside vista can be treacherous. It's like swimming backwards against the current, it's shark infested waters, it's murky and tough a times. It can also be turbulent and tricky to manoeuvre.

However, from time to time, when you experience the beautiful blue waters, with the sun shining over a secluded Caribbean bay, as everything comes together perfectly……..it makes it all worthwhile and gives it relevance and meaning."

As a friend and the current CEO of Drake & Morgan, Jillian Maclean continues to inspire, to ride out from the front and set a remarkable pace. Giving me further proof that I can improve, go faster and aspire to overtake in the future.

✕ *Change gear now and make your move out of the shadows!*

The Perfect Appetizer

On Saturday Morning Kitchen on the 8th November 2014 an Italian chef showed James Martin how his two rosetted restaurant in Italy made a signature pudding from a mistake. The error occurred when a waiter was taking the plate to a customer's table and dropped the pudding onto the kitchen floor. This gave the chef/proprietor an idea.

On the TV programme he then made the lemon centre of the pudding and rather than gently arrange this onto the flat dish he threw the filling at the plate with venom. He positioned the beautifully baked round biscuit topping on top of the mess and then cracked it with a metal spoon, thus enhancing the mistake.

Then with beautifully placed drops of potions, lotions and flavourings showing that the dish had been produced with charisma, flair and class, "the deconstructed pudding" was born!

It immediately became a talking point and because we eat with our eyes it initially appears unattractive. However, with two rosettes on the restaurants door, either the chef is insane or a mercurial genius!

What is your signature dish?

A signature dish is a recipe that identifies an individual chef. Ideally it should be unique and allow a connoisseur of good food to name the chef in a blind tasting. It can be thought of as the culinary equivalent of an artist finding their own style, or an author finding their own voice. Let's look to leave aside the main course and the dessert for now. Concentrating fully on being a small dish taken before a meal to stimulate one's appetite. It's time to become a starter!

I am often referred to by others as an entrepreneur and I have won entrepreneurial awards. It's not a title I am comfortable with or enjoy.

In fact, I believe the time has come to retire the term entrepreneur! It's outdated and loaded with baggage. It smells like a members only club, exclusive, of limited availability. It's nonsense, everyone should be encouraged to start his or her own business, not just some rare species that self-identifies as 'entrepreneurs'.

There's a new group of people out there starting businesses. They're turning profits yet never think of themselves as entrepreneurs. A lot of them don't even think of themselves as business owners. They are just doing what they love on their own terms and getting paid for it.

So let's replace the fancy sounding word with something a bit more down to earth. Instead of entrepreneurs, let's just call them **'starters.'** Anyone who creates a new business is a starter. You don't need an MBA, a certificate, a fancy suit, a briefcase or even an above average tolerance for risk. You just need an idea, a touch of confidence, a gentle nudge, although in some cases an almighty push.....to get you started!

That inspirational stimulus can arrive in numerous unexpected ways. I heard the story about Annie Downs early in 2014.

Several years ago Annie worked at the Mocha Club, a non-profit organisation based in Nashville, a group that raises money for the developing world by working with touring musicians. One day she called her boss and said something she had never said before. She stated, "I've got an idea, and I'm going to start on it tomorrow. It won't take a lot of time and it won't cost much money, and I think it's going to work."

With those two sentences, Annie changed her life. She transformed her organisation and the people it serves. She is now a professional blogger, speaker and author.

You're probably wondering what her idea was. You might even be curious about how she pulled it off. However, that would be the wrong question.

The change was in her posture. The change was that for the first time in this job, Annie wasn't waiting for instructions, working through a to-do list, or reacting to incoming tasks. She wasn't handed initiative, she took it!

Annie crossed a bridge that day. She became someone who STARTS something, someone who initiates, someone who is prepared to fail along the way if it helps her make a difference. That's a principle we believe in strongly at Victus.

Annie had a deep, intense passion and that is a great position to begin with. Turn passion on its head, instead of, "do what you love," perhaps the more effective mantra for the starter, the penalty taker and maker of change might be, "love what you do."

If we can fall in love with serving people, creating value, solving problems, building valuable connections and doing work that matters, it makes it far more likely we're going to do important work.

Imagine that the world had no middlemen, no publishers, no bosses, no HR people, no one telling you what you couldn't do.

✘ *If you lived in that world, what would you do? Well go do that - Be a Starter!*

Creating a Chocolate Heaven

Sir Alex Ferguson in his final four words of his 2013 best-selling autobiography put it well when he stated: 'It's about people's ambitions.'

- What are yours?
- How will you achieve them?
- What do they represent and look like?
- How do they manifest themselves?

In 1991 Craig Sams and Josephine Fairley established a business to support the Mayan Indians of Belize.

Its story is a heady mix of innovation, ethics, business and fair trade; in short, a great example of how to successfully launch the right product at the right time with extraordinary amounts of self-belief and passion in what you're doing.

From an original stall at the Portobello Market, London in 1991 it is estimated that the brand they created now uses a third of the world's organic cocoa. They dominate the organic chocolate market, they have an estimated 90% almighty chunk.

In 2005 the business was sold to confectionery giant Cadbury Schweppes for an estimated £20m ($36m), although it remains a stand-alone brand within the Cadbury's empire.

When it came to settling on a name, they wanted something classy, imparting a sense of confectionery history. They decided their name had to have an '&' (ampersand) in the middle.

'Green' would represent their ethical stance and 'Black' the dark, almost 'blackness' of the

70% cocoa solids in their first historic bar of chocolate. Thus, Green & Black's was born.

✘ *Discover your 'Golden Ticket'*

Pizza, Passion and Cherries

From healthy organic chocolate, to sitting eating a high calorie pizza at an airport. This recent incident in Newark with an airport cleaner had a profound effect on me. I watched as this older gentleman went to empty a large bin in the cafeteria area. He opened the door of the bin and took out the large bucket containing all the waste. He then lifted out the interior bag, tied it and threw it up on to his truck. Normally, this would be when I witness him put in a fresh bag and reposition the bucket in it's proper place.

However, I observed much more than that. That evening, I watched a professional in action. A man of principle, a man of high standards, a man who followed in the slipstream of good role models before shifting gear to overtake and become one himself. I'm sure he must have had a polka dot jersey under those work overalls!

I watched speechless, as this veteran of life then knelt down and crawled inside the empty vessel of the bin surround. He cleaned it thoroughly, disinfecting the area, mopping the floor surface, drying it all up afterwards. Then the actual bin itself got the same treatment, before having a fresh liner inserted inside and being placed back under its surround and the door being clicked shut. I sat in sheer amazement and awe at the thorough workings of this man, thinking CSI would be proud to have him.

His last touch though brightened up the remainder of my day, my week, my month. Even now as I relate this story to you, I smile and think "Could I try harder?"

This man obviously loved his work, he recognised how important it was. He was a valuable staff member, stopping problems before they began and doing a work that mattered.

Oh, his final act. He went over to the passenger seat of his van, where he had a small bag of cherries sitting. He then lifted one out, turned his head from side to side, that's when he noticed I was watching him. He then took four further steps towards his 'masterpiece,' placed the little red object on top of the bin, returned to his vehicle, looked in my direction one final time, smiled, winked at me and drove off!
Ha ha ha, he finished it off with a cherry on top. What a man, what an example, what a star.

It's okay to forgive yourself for not being the richest, the thinnest, the tallest, the one with the best hair. To forgive yourself for not being the most successful, the cutest or the one with the fastest time.

Even to forgive yourself for not winning every round or for simply being afraid.

✘ *But don't let yourself off the hook, never forgive yourself, for not caring or not trying.*

Delivering a Surprise Performance

The products and services you want to sell will not succeed in the market if you don't address the emotional wants of 'real people'. It is not enough these days just to fulfill the material needs of 'prospects'. A business (your business) needs to look past the labels it gives the people it serves, and see their hopes, dreams, fears and aspirations.

I remember watching television on the 11th of April 2009, the sniggering began as soon as the plump, matronly woman walked onto the stage.

She looked more like a lunch lady than a vocalist. First, she was too old to be competing on Britain's Got Talent, having just turned forty-seven, ten days earlier on April Fool's Day. She was more than twice the age of many of the other contestants.

But, more important, she looked, well, frumpy. The other competitors were already dressed to be the next big thing. Sexy, ruggedly handsome or hip. They wore figure hugging dresses, tailored tops and summer scarves. This woman looked more like an example of what not to wear. Her outfit looked like a cross between an old set of curtains and a secondhand Easter dress. And she was nervous.

When the judges started asking her questions, she got stuck and stumbled on her words. "What's the dream?" they inquired. When she replied that she wanted to be a professional singer you could just see the thoughts going through their heads. That's rich! You? A professional singer? The cameras zoomed in on members of the audience laughing and rolling their eyes. Even the judges smirked. They clearly wanted her to get off the stage as soon as possible.

All signs pointed to her giving a terrible performance and being booted from the show, pronto. Just when it seemed that it couldn't get any worse, she started singing.

And time stopped. It was breathtaking.

As the opening chords from "I Dreamed a Dream" from Les Miserables wafted over the speakers, Susan Boyle's exquisite voice shone

through like a beacon. So powerful, so
beautiful that it made the hair on the back of
your neck stand up. The judges were in awe,
the audience screamed and everyone broke
out into wild applause. Some started tearing
up as they listened.
The performance left people speechless.

She was a showstopper!

As of 2014 Susan Boyle had sold over 22
million albums worldwide and received two
Grammy Award nominations. Her first
appearance on Britain's Got Talent is one of
the most viral videos ever. In just nine days,
the clip accumulated more than 100 million
views. How would you like a small taste of
that kind of marketing?

It's hard to watch this video and not be
encouraged by her strength, passion and
heart. It's not only moving, it's inspiring.
She sang on behalf of everyone whose hope,
dream and aspiration it was to be on that
stage, she connected and engaged with the
viewer, and that emotion drove people to
pass it on.

This illustrates the point perfectly that when you build an audience, you don't have to buy people's attention - they give it to you.
This is a huge advantage.

Do more than 'dream the dream' - Build an audience, speak, write, blog, tweet, make videos, whatever it takes.
Share information that's valuable and you'll surely build a loyal following.

✘ *Then, when you need to get the word out, the right people will be listening.*

Statue of Liberty

Broadcast three years before I was born in 'No Mean City', the 1971 Coca-Cola 'Hilltop' advertisement is known as one of the best loved and most influential ads in TV history. It featured a multi-cultural group of teenagers singing, "I'd like to teach the world to sing (in perfect harmony)," and portrayed a positive message of hope and unity. Harvey Gabor, a member of the original creative team for the ad, says that the lines in the commercial talk about the world, however in reality it speaks to one person!

No matter what you are pitching, selling or talking about, talk to one person. You might want to appeal to a hundred, a thousand or even a million people. Do that by making your idea matter one person at a time, speak to that person, treat them well and they'll ensure that others discover you.

Interestingly, of the 146 million views generated for Coca-Cola on YouTube in 2011, only 26 million were generated by Coke, over 120 million were generated by consumers!

Often from the outside looking in, success can look easy, thinking that it happens in a moment or is catalysed by one major event.

In reality, success doesn't happen like this. For although Britain's Got Talent catapulted SuBo into the public domain, she had already jumped through plenty of hoops in pubs and clubs over the years as her apprenticeship.

Going through numerous nerve-racking auditions to eventually get before an audience of millions. I have listened to her life story on audible - The Woman I Was Born to Be, read by Elaine C. Smith.

Like so many, Susan Magdalane Boyle overcame many challenges, suffered continual setbacks and travelled down many, many roads of disappointment and discouragement before becoming 'an overnight success'.

People may forget but the last line in the song Susan Boyle sang that night: states 'Now life has killed the dream I dreamed.' In total contrast to that, let me share with you the account of how in recent years a Coca-Cola campaign tagline stated: 'Life Begins Here.' As we travel across the Atlantic in the year of 1886, and drop anchor in New York Harbour, workers were constructing the Statue of Liberty. Yet, eight hundred miles away, another great American symbol was about to be unveiled.

Like many people who change history, John Pemberton, an Atlanta pharmacist, was inspired by simple curiosity.

One afternoon, he stirred up a fragrant, caramel-coloured liquid and, when it was done, he carried it a few doors down to Jacobs' Pharmacy. Here, the mixture was combined with carbonated water and sampled by customers who all agreed - this new drink was something special.

Pemberton's bookkeeper, Frank Robinson, named the mixture and wrote it out in his distinctive script. To this day it is written the same way. In the first year, Pemberton sold just nine glasses a day. Over a century later, Coca Cola has produced more than 10's of billions of gallons of syrup.

The opportunities that you've created didn't just fall into your lap. They are not the result of one giant leap, but the product of a million tiny decisions you've been making every day for years. It is the small choices, not the momentous one-off decisions that define us.

Success is a habit. It's a daily practice of making small choices that add up in the end. It's about doing what you said you'd do, even though nobody but you will notice, and about knowing in your gut why it matters. John Pemberton and Susan Boyle can inspire us, motivate us and remind us that we each have fantastic, daily opportunities to engage with customers and fans, to enter into dialogue, to listen, to reach out to them and understand how and why they use, love or hate our product. You might have the trademark, you might even wear the crown currently, but you don't own the story. What you do have though, is an opportunity like never before to give your customers a great story to tell.

✘ *Chase those tigers, go dream your dream, be a showstopper, teach the world to sing in perfect harmony and create a monumental business. Be spurred on by curiosity and build your very own Statue of Liberty!*

Polka Dot, It Suits You

These days tourists and holiday makers travel from all over the world to visit both the Statue of Liberty and the Eiffel tower. Over a century ago, however, when two brothers decided to publish a guide for French motorists, there were fewer than 3,000 cars in France.

The directory was intended to boost demand for vehicles. They had nearly 35,000 copies printed in 1900. It was then given away free of charge. It contained useful information for motorists, including maps, instructions for repairing and changing tyres, lists of car mechanics, hotels and petrol stations. Four years later the siblings published a similar publication for Belgium.

In 2013 it was published in 14 editions and sold in nearly 90 countries.

Forenames of those enterprising brothers: Andre and Edouard. *The Michelin Guide was born!*

What goes hand in hand with what you currently do that could increase turnover? That if created, produced or delivered, would power, propel and 'drive' people toward your business?

French chef Paul Bocuse, one of the pioneers of nouvelle cuisine in the 1960s, said, "Michelin is the only guide that counts." In France, each year, at the time the guide is published, it sparks a media frenzy which has been compared to that for annual Academy Awards for films.

Media debate likely winners, speculation is rife, and TV and newspapers discuss which restaurant might lose, and who might gain, a Michelin star.

The Michelin Guide also awards Rising Stars, an indication that a restaurant has the potential to qualify for a star, or an additional star. The term "Michelin Star" is a hallmark of fine dining quality and restaurants around the world tout their Michelin Star status. Celebrity chef Gordon Ramsay cried when the Michelin Guide stripped the stars from his New York restaurant, calling the food "erratic". Ramsay explained that failing to retain the stars was like "losing a girlfriend." Of course, the hilarious part of all of this is that this prestigious restaurant rating is from................. a tyre company!

Take time to recognise the rising stars within your industry, both at national and local level. On a daily basis, whose slipstream do you sit in? Who continually stretches you to go faster, to become better, who generates in you that passion and belief to be a person of influence?

Today is when you to stride out confidently on to that stage alongside Susan Boyle, you step forward and produce the goods. The apprentice, trainee or novice title is long gone. You are no longer an up-and-coming hopeful, but a trailblazer, a catalyst and a doer. An individual of presence, substance and integrity. Ease out from the shadows, continue to climb upwards, put on your polka dot jersey and become 'The King of the Mountains' ....

✘ *Go conquer the world!*

Ask the Question

Speaking of rising stars, it has been said that after meeting with the legendary British Prime Minister William Gladstone, you left feeling he was the smartest person in the world, but after meeting with his rival Benjamin Disraeli, you left thinking you were!

The premise of this book is simple. You can create genius around you and receive a higher contribution from your people.
My good friend Michael Patterson who has helped me co-author this work, wrote a terrific short, yet insightful business book in 2013 entitled Time For Kick-Off: Succeeding in Business and in Life, When the Whistle Blows! It's a fascinating, entertaining footballing parable all about making the most of our lives, fulfilling our potential and achieving our goals.

The key take away from it for me, was about being a Penalty Taker. A Penalty Taker you may have guessed is an individual that inspires and leads from the front, that is willing to step forward, and take responsibility. Victus helps create individuals known for their leadership skills, work ethic and their personal integrity. They develop others, they stir emotions, they receive what money can't buy and strive continually to make the world a better place!

In most, but not all businesses that I do consultancy work for, there are Penalty Takers. People who attract the best talent (source prime ingredients), harness it fully and prepare it for the next stage. These leaders have a reputation not only for delivering results, but for creating a place where young, talented individuals can grow. Victus can help you fulfill that potential, enable you to move on to the next level and become that Michelin rising star!

Perhaps you are already a Penalty Taker? Would your people describe you as someone who recognises talented people, draws them in and utilises them well? Would they say they have grown more around you than with any other manager they have worked for? Look to operate as a Penalty Taker. They attract talented people and deploy them well.

You might think of it as working at their highest point of contribution. They get access to the best talent, not because they are necessarily great recruiters, but rather because people clamour to work for them.

That cycle of attraction begins with a leader possessing the confidence and magnetism to surround him or herself with "quality players." Under the tutelage of a Penalty Taker, the genius of these players gets discovered, experience is gained and maturity develops. Having been stretched, these players become smarter and more capable. Lower league players become Championship standard.

Championship players grow, blossom and develop into Premiership class. These people are positioned in the spotlight and get kudos and recognition for their work. They attract attention and their value increases in the talent market-place, internally or externally. These, now Premiership rated players get offered even bigger opportunities and seize them with the full support of the Penalty Taker.

As this wonderful pattern of utilisation, growth and opportunity occurs across multiple people, others in the organisation notice.....and the leader and the company get a reputation. They build a name for themselves as "the place to grow."

This reputation spreads and more top players flock to work in the Penalty Takers organisation, so there is always a steady flow of talent in the door, replacing the flourishing talent growing out of the organisation.

✗ *As you look to gain your 'Michelin Star', do you inspire, enthuse and empower people to do their best work? Are you a Gladstone or Disraeli?*

Knightsbridge & Kevin Bridges

Hitesh Patel did not wear a polka dot shirt when we last met, but he is certainly conquering the catering world.

In mid September 2014, I had a meeting in Covent Garden, a district in London on the eastern fringes of the West End. When I won my scholarship - I got to go work for a company called Paperchase. Paperchase are Europes largest hospitality accountancy firm. It was Hitesh who, along with his two brothers Aku and Minesh set up the firm. I met him in an office block above a launderette in Sydenham Road, London. The story began with him doing his own financial returns. Then he started doing the accounts and providing conventional bookkeeping services to others, although mostly to restaurants. It became bigger and bigger and bigger.

I said to him, "Hitesh, do you do much work in Scotland? thinking I was 'Charlie Big Potato,' you know, as if I had this huge multi-national brand on the go.

"No," he replied, "we don't do anything in Scotland." I responded with, "Oh, that's right, so you're just a small company?"

Hitesh, as a humble man, enlightened me. "Not exactly, we look after over seventy-five restaurant clients with offices in London, New York, Miami, Hong Kong and Dubai.

We have over a hundred staff in India and forty plus in the United Kingdom."

"Okay." I sheepishly said, "Who do you look after?"

Hitesh then rhymed off nearly every major restauranteur in London, including Philip Howard, Bruce Poole and Heston Blumenthal.

I'd kept in touch with Paperchase. They'd invited me to lunch this day. They wanted to catc.h up, and had some things to ask me. I had met one of the men before, Mr Desailly, a Kenyan. However, the other man, an Indian gentleman was new to me. I walked in and thought I'll do the ice breaker.

"There's a joke here boys, definitely a joke." They both looked at each other across the table and quipped, "What do you mean there is a joke?" To which this cheeky visiting Glaswegian boldly states in a broad Kevin Bridges accent,

"There is a Kenyan, an Indian and a Scotsman and they all sit down for a curry!" Silence....

As the lunch began, they asked if I would mind them selecting for me, as they said they would have been willing to take 'counsel' from myself if they had came north of the border. "Let us order the food," they insisted.

It was a Tapas lunch, a bit of this, a bit of that and a bit of the next thing. "You're a big hardy Scot Andrew, do you think you can handle the spice?" they questioned. My honour was at stake, my national pride, my self esteem, "I can handle spice." I spluttered, before I really knew the rules of the game.

These guys were getting the Nan bread, wiping down the plate like professional window cleaners removing soapy suds from a pane of glass, scraping it artistically deep into into the corners of the square shaped bowl, sourcing taste from every nook and cranny!

Me, the 6ft 6in 'hardy Scot,' I had a mini Niagara Falls cascading down my forehead. I was crying over lunch, people at the other tables must have thought I'd received heartbreaking news!

The heat from those curries was intense, I'm talking pain with a capital P. It was a slow, severe, measured torture. I thought they don't want to question me about anything, they want to do me harm. They are going to interrogate me and this is how they'll break me. At this point I'd own up to anything. I decided to speak, but I couldn't, my vocal chords had returned to Glasgow all on their own. I was defeated. The will to live was gone.

I remember physically putting a loo roll in the fridge that night in preparation for the following day. Not sure what brand, but I'm sure it was 'soft, strong and very, very long!' When I met Hitesh previously as part of my scholarship, he was working in an office that I walked past regularly. I gave him a few minutes of my time most days and we struck up a bit of a bond. Now a few years later, he'd phoned and said, "Remember how we met, how we became friends, when are you next down in London? Allow me to take you to lunch, introduce you to some friends and treat you to a curry!" Remind me never to answer his calls ever again!

At Victus, we encourage you to make some sound investments - ideally in locations, in surroundings, and in products. Also in future planning and in personal goals.

Predominantly, though you should be investing in people! Having a share in, backing and underwriting peoples individual pursuits, their hopes, aims and desires.

There is always an opportunity to learn from all those who cross our path.

- Good people bring you happiness.
- Bad ones give you experience.
- The worst ones give you lessons
- The best ones present you with lifelong memories.

✘ *Don't regret knowing the people that come into your life.*

In Bed with Timeless

Lifelong memories, a substantial period of time, longevity and durability, the very essence of a successful company. The core of your business should be built around things that won't change.

Things that people are going to want today and ten years from now. Those are things pivotal to your growth.

Amazon focuses on fast (or free) shipping, great selection, friendly return policies and affordable prices. These things will always be in high demand. Japanese car makers also focus on core principles that don't change: reliability, affordability and practicality. People wanted those things thirty years ago, they want them today and they'll want them thirty years in the future.

✘ *Remember, fashion fades away. When you focus on permanent features, you're in bed with things that never go out of style.*

A Genuine Dish Worth Sharing

You will be aware of Delia Smith, Jamie Oliver and Rick Stein. What about Raymond Blanc and the Hairy Bikers? They are all great chefs, but there are plenty of terrifically talented chefs out there. So why do you know these few better than others?
It's because they share everything they know. They put their recipes in publications and deliver their techniques on cookery shows. They do radio programmes, interviews and appear on TV.

As a business owner, you should share everything you know too. This is an often alien and foreign concept to most in the business world. Businesses are usually paranoid and secretive. They think they have proprietary THIS and competitive advantage THAT. Maybe a rare few do, but most don't. Those that don't should stop acting like those that do. Don't be afraid of sharing. A recipe is much easier to copy than a business. Shouldn't that scare the celebrity TV chef?

Why would he or she go on television and show you how he does what he does? Why would he put all his recipes in written format where anyone can buy and then replicate them? Because he knows those recipes and techniques are not enough to beat him at his own game. No one's going to buy his latest bestseller, open a restaurant next door and put him out of business.

It just doesn't work like that. Yet this is what many in the business world think will happen if their competitors learn how they do things. Get over it.

Go out there and emulate those famous chefs. They cook, make public appearances and they write. What do you do? What are your 'recipes'? What can you tell the world about how you operate that's informative, educational and promotional?

✘ *This book is my cookbook. Where is yours?*

Get Your 5 a Day

In recent years the Adidas Innovation Team, the AIT as they refer to themselves, developed one of their most innovative products so far.

They enhanced their highly successful and popular Predator range of football boot. They added lethal zone technology.

A football match is 90 minutes long. Broken down, statistics show that is equivalent to each player being on the ball for 90 seconds, which equates to roughly 60-80 ball contacts. It means every touch you have on the ball needs to count!

They pinpointed Dribble; First Touch; Sweet Spot; Control & Pass and Drive as the 5 crucial areas.

The key quote from Adidas was, "The players have to be behind the concept; live the concept and ultimately love the concept!"

In the food industry, I would identify them thus:

Dribble - To produce or present succulent, delectable, luscious mouth watering food.

First Touch - The idea behind that is, you eat with your eyes. It's in the presentation, it's appearance, that when food is brought out you think, "That looks delicious!"

Sweet Spot - Gregg Wallace, turning the spoon with passion. On Masterchef if it was an average pudding, the spoon would go in, he'd take a bite and bring it back out stating, "That was alright," then he would comment on it. If it was a dessert that was extraordinarily tasteful, the spoon would go in, it would slowly twist in his mouth, he would ease it steadily back out upside down. Then you'd witness him almost 'pop' with happiness.

Control & Pass - Is about handling how you engage with the customer. Quickly they form opinions, either negative or positive. If they leave and they've now taken a leaflet, a business card, a flyer, or perhaps they've rebooked to come back, they didn't know you did outdoor catering or afternoon tea, but now they do. Then you've up sold, you've courtesy checked, you've 'controlled' the whole experience and 'passed' the test.

Drive - By doing all of the above exceedingly well....... you will 'drive' customers/clients to return regularly.

✘ *Identify your Lethal Zones?*

Gibraltar Kev

Recently on holiday in Gibraltar I was 'driven' around by a taxi driver called Gibraltar Kev. I said to Kev, "Where are you from?" He replied, "I'm born and bred in Gibraltar, I'm a Gibraltarian. I speak Spanish and English, so I speak Spanglish."

He then told me, "Thirty-thousand people live in Gibraltar, but every day six thousand people travel across the border from Spain to work there also. The Spanish don't want people leaving Spain to go to Gibraltar, the English don't want people leaving to go into Spain, it is a nightmare." I said to him, "right, so obviously you can live here because you are a Gibraltarian, you have a home and you have a family?"

"Yes, and for my holidays I cross the border and go into Spain," he said. I asked, "Have you ever gone further afield than Spain?" "Why would I?" he responded. "I live in Gibraltar, if I ever want to go abroad, I go 100 metres that way into Spain, and I'm abroad. I've done my holidays, why would I go anywhere else?"

You think, simple! "Sometimes, is it not the richest man who is the man that needs the least, and not the man who has got the most?"
So does that not just underline the fact that he is super content. What one man wants, another man doesn't. People probably aspire to have a fraction of what you and I have got, but then you and I still want blah, blah, blah. It's the fact that he was so content, and the fact that he looked at me like he was confused, the fact I questioned, "Why do you never go abroad?"
"I do go abroad, I go across there, that's abroad, that's Spain, I live in Gibraltar!

✘ *The power of contentment.*

Becoming Einstein

Albert Einstein was not as contented as Gibraltar Kev, in fact he was the polar opposite. He continually aspired for more and he excelled in numeracy.

Mathematics is a field that many people shy away from, but there are some who had a passion for numbers and making discoveries regarding equations, measurements, and other numerical solutions in history. They looked for ways to understand the world as it relates to numbers and their contributions have been very important for their generation and beyond.

Do you have a marketing department? If not, good!

If you do, don't think these are the only people responsible for marketing. Accounting is a department. Marketing is not. Marketing is something everyone in your company is doing 24/7/365.

Just as you cannot not communicate, you cannot not market.

- Every time you answer the phone, it's marketing.
- Every time you send an email, it's marketing.
- Every time someone uses your product, it's marketing.
- Every word you write on your website is marketing.

If you're in the restaurant business, the after dinner mint is marketing! Recognise that all of these little things are more important and more precious to your name, than choosing which piece of promotional tat to throw into a conference goodie bag.

Don't be afraid to give a little away for free - As long as you've got something else to sell. Be confident in what you're offering. You should know that people will come back for more. If you're not confident about that, you haven't created a strong enough product.

✘ *Become Einstein, be a mathematician, for marketing isn't just a few individual events, it is the sum total of everything you do*

Employ a Goalkeeper

My oldest boy, Cammy (Cameron), does not get too excited yet at the prospect of doing his Maths homework, but boy, does he love his football. He's a goalie. I watch him regularly stand in the centre of his goal with his 'sooper dooper' extra large gloves. Gloves that are nearly as big as his face.

If you were a goalkeeper, you wouldn't apply to be a forward for a football club, because you're a goalie. You've got the proper tools - the over sized gloves, the elbow pads and the obligatory towel to place in the back of the net!

So, do what you do.

Do it well and do it properly!

Wherever the foundation of your business is, focus there. If you've got a tiny electrical goods store or a chain of independent travel agents, make them the kind of place that people seek out and want to come back to.

If I look to employ your daughter and she's a student at University wanting a summer job and has also applied to Top Shop, Asda and Primark. I offer her a role at a Heaven Scent Coffee Shop, doing 16 hours a week. When she starts I put her in the kitchen to do 2 eight hour shifts. A couple of weeks later I speak to the manager and mention,
"That new girl that's in the kitchen, she is not really doing the right GP, the cost of sales are not worked out properly, her food presentation is not very good, and I blame him.

In his defence, he rightly states, "What you are doing is simply filling the void of a position with anybody, as opposed to holding off and getting the right person who is specific, qualified and trained for that task!"

Relating back to the Drake & Morgan story. If you wanted to be a barman with them, they'd do working interviews, expect you to have a wealth of experience in the drinks industry and you'd have to have a huge knowledge of cocktails, or else you are a guy who likes a drink......you are NOT a barman!

If you are a chef, then be passionate about food, talk about food, let me see you cook. I employ several waiters in my businesses.

They are all superb waiters, they applied to be waiters and that is what they do. I can monitor them, judge them and assess them doing the job they were employed to do.....they are not filling a gap!

✗ *Where do you position your business?*

Best Before

We all have ideas. Ideas are immortal. What doesn't last forever is inspiration. Inspiration is like fresh fruit or milk, it has an expiry date.

If you want to do something, you've got to do it now. You can't wait two months to get around to it. You can't just say you'll do it later. Later, you won't be pumped up about it anymore.

If you are inspired on a Friday, write off the weekend and dive into the project. When you are high on inspiration, you can get two week's worth of work done in twenty-four hours. Inspiration is a time machine in that way.

Inspiration is a magical thing, a productivity multiplier, a motivator. Alas, it won't wait for you however. Inspiration is a now thing. If it grabs you, grab it right back and put it to work.

✘ *Put the book down, email me and let's create an exciting project together....NOW!*

The Winner Is

Far from the eagerly anticipated and globally televised event it is today, the first Academy Awards ceremony took place out of the public eye (in the slipstream) during an Academy banquet at the Hollywood Roosevelt Hotel. Two hundred and seventy people attended the May 16th 1929 dinner in the hotel's Blossom Room.

There was little suspense when the awards were presented that night, as the recipients

had already been announced three months earlier!
Since 2001, the Oscar ceremony has been held in Hollywood's Dolby Theatre and in 2014 the 86th Annual Academy Awards had a total viewership of 43.7 million.

As a glamorous star of stage and screen strolls out to the podium, they briefly pause, before informing us of all the nominees for the particular category. We then view selected clips from each of their movies before the audience is hushed, the celebrity holds up and opens the envelope and announces: The winner is... wait, hold up, stop or in cinematic terms let's rewind.

First ask, how do you get nominated and make it onto that prized shortlist?
Shortlists, many industries have one.

As a young singer you may be sitting around the table with your manager chatting about your next song and someone suggests, "Maybe we could get Paulo Nutini to write it?" The ad agency and the client are discussing the new campaign, and inevitably, someone says, "Maybe Nigella Lawson could

be our spokesperson?" With Noel Edmunds to chair, Andy Murray to endorse, Duncan Bannatyne to invest, you get the idea.
In business often the shortlist consists of the esteemed obvious choices, the people who are seen as making it all come together.
So, again, how do you get on THAT shortlist?

After all, once you are on the shortlist, not only do your fees quadruple, but the amount of work increases to the point where you can't possibly do it all. Like we mentioned previously, it's easy to seduce yourself into thinking it's a straight up meritocracy. The funniest comedians, the most talented chefs, the most impactful speakers - these gifted individuals are chosen for the shortlist because they deserve it.

Except that is not correct.

Yes, of course, you need a minimum amount of talent to make the shortlist. It might even help to be a genius. Nonetheless, plenty of people with talent (and plenty of geniuses) aren't there, aren't thought of by industry outsiders and those looking for a straightforward way to bring on someone they can trust.

No, the shortlist requires more than that. Luck, sure, but also the persistence of doing the work in the right place in the right way for a very long time. Not an overnight success, but one that took a decade or three.

The secret of getting on the shortlist is doing your best work fearlessly for a long time before you get on the list, and (especially) doing it even if you are not on the list!

Glenn Close has been on the Oscar shortlist six times but has yet to win. In 2012 though, the Academy named Christopher Plummer, at age 82, as the Best Actor in a Supporting Role, he became the oldest winner in any acting category for his performance in Beginners (which he obviously is not).

As he clutched his statuette, the debonaire thespian addressed it thus: "You're only two years older than me darling, where have you been all of my life?"

Plummer had been in the industry for over 60 years building his audience.

Trade the dream of instant success for slow, measured growth. It can be hard, but you have to be patient, stick with it, you have to be willing to grind it out. You often have to do it for a long time before the right people notice. Again, once you have some customers and a history, you'll have a story to tell. Just launching isn't a good story. Continue to get people interested in what you have to say. And then keep at it.

✘ *In time you'll get to have the last laugh when people discuss your "overnight" success!*

Shaken Not Stirred

Continuing with the acting theme - nearly two decades ago, I was a twenty-two year old James Bond wannabee. Waking up in a room overlooking the largest inland stretch of water in Great Britain, I throw back the Egyptian cotton bed sheet, stumble across the room, and pull back the curtains to take in the beautiful scenic view over Loch Lomond in West Dunbartonshire.

I venture downstairs, through the car park, past my Porsche 924 and Honda Fireblade Motorcycle. I've got a White Lightning boat and a Jet Ski. I've got an extensive wine and whisky knowledge, get a full English breakfast seven days a week and eat like a King.

Yet, six years previously at High School the teacher told me, "You will either go to prison or end up a bum." An interesting career choice I was offered!

The Inverbeg Inn is located on the shores of the Loch. I worked six days a week, the money I earned I simply banked it, banked it, banked it. I just bought nice things. For although I had a flat in Glasgow, I was never there, I just rented it out.
Occasionally I'd go back between tenants. I was living rent free, I was on good money and I ate and drank out of the hotel.

Ultimately my choice on this rare day off is to go back to my residence in Glasgow or stay in my flat overlooking the loch?
I could phone a friend who'd come up in their luxury yacht, we'd go out fishing, drink some fine wine and eat some fancy cuisine. Choices, choices.

I now have none of that. I am now the keeper of my own destiny, for it was all mirrored, it was false. For every minute I was there, the person was buying my time, as opposed to buying my experience. I was getting one day off per week. So although it looked very grand on the surface, there was huge underlying issues.

The awakening dawned on me one day at a quarterly meeting in the boardroom of 8 St. Andrews Square, Edinburgh, in the heart of the capital. I sat at one end of a rather imposing 20ft mahogany table. Two high chairs at the executive end and one definitely smaller and armless chair at the other.

"Andrew, how is your performance?" the voice bellowed from the opposite side of the room. "How are the recent facts and figures for the past quarter? How are your like for like sales compared to last year?"

They would want you to spend money on things that were irrelevant, but then not spend on 'incidentals', like...looking after the customer!

At this particular meeting in the Head Office they mentioned in a matter of fact way, "Andrew, when you get to sixty, you want to have yourself a yacht!" - I thought super, smashing, here I am with my company car - a battered old Ford Escort, number plate N653 ASC sitting double parked outside, no doubt with a ticket, dent in the wing-mirror, quarter tank of fuel, having travelled through from Loch Lomond, and they tell me this.

I asked the CEO, "do you have a yacht?" He pondered, he thought about it, then he looked up and said, "Aye, I think it may be in Helensburgh." I thought, YOU THINK it may be in Helensburgh...............time for me to move on!

I chose to relinquish the Porsche, the Jet Ski, Boat and Motorbike, I sold them all. I became a starter that day.

I invested in myself and opened my first Heaven Scent Coffee Shop. (I wish I had bought a large bag of cherries also).

I changed gears, I moved out of the shadows and began constructing my own 'Scott Monument.' I experienced freedom for the first time that day.

I was also intrigued to know how much it costs to berth a yacht at a marina.

✗ *Is today the day you take that "monumental" step?*

Happy New Year

Ty Warner built an empire on stuffed toys and in January 2014 he narrowly escaped a prison sentence. The 69-year-old Chicago billionaire was fined, given two years of probation and 500 hours of community service for tax evasion. In fairness he had already paid a civil penalty of $53 million, plus back taxes.

Beanie Babies began to emerge as popular collectibles in late 1995, and became a hot toy. The company's strategy of deliberate scarcity, producing each new design in limited quantity, restricting individual store shipments to limited numbers of each design and regularly retiring designs, created a huge secondary market for the toys and increased their popularity and value as a collectible. I was a collector!

Meeting up with Greg Wallis (a different one) of Tower Records in Chicago on one of my visits to the States, he says to me, "Andrew, you know there is a new craze about to sweep the world. It is called Beanie Babies made by a company called TY, the guy is from Chicago and McDonalds are starting to get into it."

Unlike Cabbage Patch Dolls which had gone before, and were more gift priced at around the £15.00 mark, Beanie Babies were affordable, within the pocket money range at between £2.99 and £4.99.

Greg had told me that there were a dozen available. He gave me a gift of all twelve to take home and advised me to do nothing with them!

So as a grown man, twenty-three years of age, I packed my suitcase with an assorted selection of these cuddly toys. I brought them home, straight through customs, to their new habitat in Bonnie Scotland, no passports, visas or anything.

On returning I was told that Pickwicks in Edinburgh were selling them. I jump in the car, travel East and upon arrival ask the lady behind the counter, "Do you sell Beanie Babies?" "Yes," she replied politely, "we have eight different ones and we have four of each." "Brilliant, I'll take all thirty-two please," I said excitedly.

"What," she exclaimed. With a huge grin on my face I responded, "Yep, I'll take them all." Now remember that this is before the Internet. I started hoarding, hoarding, hoarding 'rawhide' Beanie Babies. Did I mention I hoarded them?

Other stores started selling them and I took them all! A place in the Buchanan Galleries shopping arcade in Glasgow began stocking them...I took them all.

A friend started working in the toy department at John Lewis in Glasgow. He phoned me up to say, "Beanie Babies are now everywhere, then his voice dropped into secret agent mode.

He began to whisper softly and I could picture him looking from side to side as he told me in slow hushed tones, "we have Britannia Bear!"

Now Britannia Bear was the most sought after of them all. "How many do you have?" I immediately asked him. "Three," he replied in his now official MI6 voice.

I could hear the theme tune to Mission Impossible playing on a loop, within ten minutes I had arrived at my destination. John Lewis were only allowed to sell one per person. So I got the first one, went out, came back in and bought number two. I then repeated the step one more time, Tom Cruise would have been extremely proud, mission accomplished!

A few years passed, it would now be around 1999, eBay and the Internet are thriving and I have accrued approximately two and a half thousand Beanie Babies, yes 2500 assorted cuddly toys are in my official warehouse (mum and dad's garage).

I started to buy and sell them. I traded in official TY BB's. I was the 'Arfur' Daley of the Beanie World, the Beanmeister, the head Bean counter, Beanz Meanz Money....so I SOLD OUT!!!!

They paid for my boat, my Jet Ski and my next two trips to Chicago.

Proud to be British………"Rule Britannia Bear!"

✘ *Scarcity drives demand for your products and services*

Once Upon a Time

From Britannia Bear, to Goldilocks and the Three Bears, stories carry things.

A lesson or moral. Information or a take-home message.

Take my boys most loved nursery rhyme, the famous tale of "The Three Little Pigs." Three brothers leave home to head into the world to seek their fortune. The first little pig quickly builds his house out of straw. The second pig as we know used sticks. Both throw their houses together as quickly as possible so they can hang out and play the rest of the day. The third pig however, is more disciplined. He takes the time and effort to carefully build his house out of bricks, even while his brothers have fun around him.

One night, a big bad wolf comes along looking for something to eat. He goes to the first pig's house and says those words so beloved by small children: "Little pig, little pig, let me in."

But when the pig says no, the wolf blows the pig's house down. He does the same to the house of sticks. But when the wolf tries the same thing at the third pig's house, it doesn't work. He huffs and he puffs but the wolf can't destroy the third pig's house because it's made of bricks.

And that is the moral of the story. Effort pays off, build solid foundations, make the investment, take the time to do things right. You might not have as much fun right away, but you'll find that it's worth it in the end.

✗ *Stories give people freedom to come to their own conclusions.*

Ssshh

I love America, the East Coast in particular. Let me share with you a rather lengthy, but highly interesting story not often heard, rarely spoken about and a real hidden gem.

Among the brownstones and vintage shops on St. Mark's Place near Tompkins Square Park in New York City, you'll notice a small eatery. It's marked by a large red hot-dog-shaped sign with the words "eat me" written on what looks like mustard. Walk down a small flight of stairs and you're in a genuine old hole-in-the-wall hot dog restaurant. The long tables are set with all your favourite condiments, you can play any number of arcade-style video games, and, of course, order off a menu to die for.

Seventeen varieties of hot dogs are offered. Every type of frankfurter you could imagine. The Good Morning is a bacon wrapped hot dog smothered with melted cheese and topped with a fried egg. The Tsunami has teriyaki, pineapple and green onions. Purists can order the New Yorker, a classic grilled all-beef frankfurter.

But look beyond the gingham tablecloths and hipsters enjoying their dogs. Notice that vintage wooden phone booth tucked into the corner? The one that looks like something Clark Kent might have dashed into to change into Superman? Go ahead, peek inside.

You'll notice an old-school rotary dial phone hanging on the inside of the booth, the type that has a finger wheel with little holes for you to dial each number. Just for kicks, place your finger in the hole under the number 2 (ABC). Dial clockwise until you reach the finger stop, release the wheel, and hold the receiver to your year.

To your astonishment, someone answers. "Do you have a reservation?" a voice asks. "A reservation," "yes, a reservation." Of course you don't have one. What would you even need a reservation for? A phone booth in the corner of a hot dog restaurant?

Today however, is your lucky day, apparently they can take you. Suddenly, the back of the booth swings open - its a secret door!!! - and you are let into a clandestine bar called, of all things, Please Don't Tell.

What an amazing story. Having made further enquiries, I discovered that back in 1999, Brian Shebairo and his childhood friend Chris Antista decided to get into the hot dog business. The pair had grown up in New Jersey eating at famous places like Rutt's Hut and Johnny & Hanges and wanted to bring that same hot dog experience to New York City.

After two full years of R & D, riding their motorcycles up and down the East Coast tasting the best hot dogs, Brian and Chris were ready. On October 6th, 2001, they opened Crif Dogs in the East Village. What kind of name is that I hear you ask, well it came from the sound that poured out of Brian's mouth one day when he tried to say Chris's name while still munching on a hot dog. Brilliant!

Crif Dogs was a big hit and won the best hot dog award from a variety of publications. As the years passed, Brian was looking for a new challenge.

He wanted to open a bar. Crif Dogs had always had a drinks license but had never taken full advantage of it. He and Chris had experimented with a frozen margarita machine, and kept a bottle of Jagermeister in the freezer occasionally, but to do it right they really needed more space. Next door was a struggling tea lounge. Brian's lawyer said that if they could get the space, the license would transfer. After three years of constant prodding, the neighbour finally gave in.

But now the tough part. New York City is flush with bars. In a four block radius around Crif Dogs there are more than sixty places to grab a drink. A handful are even on the same block.

Originally, Brian had a grungy rock and roll bar in mind. But that wouldn't cut it. The concept needed to be something more remarkable. Something that would get people talking and draw them in.

One day Brian ran into a friend who had an antique business. A big outdoor flea market selling everything from art deco dressers to glass eyes and stuffed cheetahs! The guy said he had just found a neat old 1930's phone booth that he thought would work well in Brian's bar.

Brian had an idea. When he was a kid, his uncle worked as a carpenter. In addition to helping to build houses and the usual things that carpenters do, the uncle built a room in the basement that had secret doors. The doors weren't even that concealed, just wood that meshed into other wood, but if you pushed in the right place, you could get

access to a hidden storage space. No secret lair or loot concealed inside, but cool nonetheless.
Brian decided to turn the phone booth into the door to a secret bar!

Everything about Please Don't Tell suggests that you've been let into a very special secret. You won't find a sign posted on the street. You won't find it advertised on billboards or in magazines. The only entrance is through a semi-hidden phone booth inside a hot dog diner.

Of course, this makes no sense. Don't marketers preach that blatant advertising and easy access are the cornerstones of a successful business?

Please Don't Tell has never advertised. Yet since opening in 2007 it has been one of the most sought-after drink reservations in New York City. It takes bookings only the day of, and the reservation line opens at 3.00pm sharp.

Spots are first-come, first-served. Callers madly hit redial again and again in the hopes of cutting through the busy signals. By 3.30pm all spots are booked.

Please Don't Tell doesn't push market. It doesn't try to hustle you in the door or sell you with a flashy website. It's a classic "discovery brand."

Whisper it: the Heaven Scent Coffee Shop in Milnathort, Kinross, also has a secret space, access is gained through the refrigerator in the seating area. Ssshh!

✖ *The most powerful marketing is personal recommendation. Nothing is more viral or infectious than one of your friends going to a place and giving it his full recommendation. And what could be more remarkable than watching two people disappear into the back of a phone booth?*

Inside the Kitchen

Give people a backstage pass and show them how your business works. Imagine that someone wanted to make a reality show about your business. What would they share? Now stop waiting for someone else and do it yourself.

Think no one will care? Think again. Even seemingly boring jobs can be fascinating when presented correctly.

People are curious about how things are made. It's why they like factory tours or behind-the-scenes footage on DVDs. They want to see how the sets are built, how the animation is done, how the director cast the film, etc. They want to know how and why other people make decisions!

You see, letting people behind the curtain changes your relationship with them. They'll feel a bond with you and see you as a human being instead of a faceless company. They'll see the sweat and effort that goes into what you sell. They'll develop a deeper level of understanding and appreciation for what you do.

Don't worry about how you're supposed to sound and how you are supposed to act.

Show the world what you're really like, warts and all.

There's a beauty to imperfection. This is the essence of the Japanese principle of Wabi-Sabi. Wabi-Sabi values character and uniqueness over a shiny facade. It teaches that cracks and scratches in things should be embraced. It's also about simplicity. You strip things down and then like being on Ready Steady Cook, you use what you have available to you.

Leonard Koren, an author of a book on Wabi-Sabi, gives this advice, he says "Pare down to the essence, but don't remove the poetry. Keep things clean and unencumbered but don't sterilise." It's a beautiful way to put it, 'leave the poetry in what you make.' For when it becomes too polished, it loses it's soul.

✘ *So talk like you really talk. Reveal things that others are unwilling to discuss. Be upfront about your shortcomings. Show the latest version of what you're working on, even if you're not done yet. It's okay if it's not perfect. You might not seem as professional, but you will seem a lot more sincere...a genuine dish worth sharing!*

Become a Master of Cheese

Now here is a dish worth sharing.

When I was at The Inverbeg Inn celebrating the Millennium, we had just received another 4 star tourist board grading again and the owners had said, "take yourself, plus one, out for a nice slap up meal at our expense, enjoy your evening."

My younger brother Graham who was working alongside me as a trainee manager, was my chosen guest for the evening. We took ourselves along to the Michelin starred Amaryllis (restaurant) in Glasgow, at that point run by Gordon Ramsay. Ramsay was high profile, he had the Boiling Point TV series, where he'd walked out of a top London restaurant and taken his entire team with him. He is now going into kitchens kicking off! "I don't get these from NOT doing 20 hours a day working," he'd yell, pointing at his big frown lines highlighted by the cameras.

In his 2006 'Humble Pie' autobiography he admits it didn't work. He tried to bring London to Glasgow, the 1990 European City of Culture was still not ready for it!

The location was at One Devonshire Gardens, it had no number outside and you entered through a doorway just off Great Western Road. You then continued down a building or two in this rather imposing Victorian townhouse in Glasgow's fashionable West End.

We walked along the corridor and entered the next room. We looked and felt.....'out of place.'

There we were, two guys from the Southside walking in thinking, "this is a wee bit daunting, this is very posh." The maitre d' takes your jacket and escorts you into this huge, big palatial dining room. It has the finest linen, over sized wine glasses, cutlery as big as your hands.....amazing, simply stunning!

It was a set menu and was something like eighty or ninety pounds a head or thereabouts. It doesn't matter, it was not inexpensive.

A seven course tasting menu - So out comes this small dribble, on a pool of, enhanced with, accompanied by?

You manage all that with one bite thinking, smashing and that's it gone!

Then out comes a petite amuse-bouche, which amused my mouth, as the literal translation would suggest.

Then comes a gazpacho cold soup, followed by a fish course, a main course, then a pudding - and there is still one course to go.

The waiter approaches us and says, "would anyone like to see the Cheese Master?" "Let me just stop you there my friend, the what, the Cheese Master?" The waiter says, "Yes, we have a Master of Cheese." My brother then cries, "wow, wow, wow, seriously, you have a Master of Cheese? You have somebody who specializes in cheese?"

So, sure enough in he comes, this large imposing gent with an all in one tabard and goatee beard. He glides effortlessly towards us with the trolley, stops just short of our table and says, "Good evening gentlemen, may I give you a guided tour of the board?"

We both looked at each other excitedly and stated in brotherly unison, with our very best Newton Mearns accent, "A guided tour of the board, don't mind if you do!"

He then enthusiastically went on to educate us on everything he had. "This is a Caboc, dating from the fifteenth century in the Scottish Highlands, or how about Chhurpi, it's a Tibetan Yak cheese, this one is twelve per cent 'whatever,' from the hills of 'wherever.' We also do a Yugoslavian 'such and such,' from the caves of 'blah,blah,blah,' it's hand mined in, etc, etc, etc.

We both thought brilliant, amazing, out of this world. We could point to a cheese and this guy could tell us where it came from, how it was made, the process, the storage, how it managed to be in front of us right now, the whole shebang. He was a family history expert...in cheese, he knew its parents, grandparents and all its siblings. He was indeed a Cheese Master.

After working his way around the whole board, he says, "Gentlemen, any preference?" To which my brothers considered response was, "Yes..........any Babybel?"

*****

My brother Graham died prematurely on the 24th January 2011.

Dollars, Euros, Ideas & Pounds

Ideas are the new social currency, ideas can transform your business overnight. Take time to review, reflect and discuss them, throw them off each other, at doorways, floors and walls.......see what sticks, what feels right.

Explore it further, move it forward, give it arms and legs, care for it, nurture it and allow it to grow. Watch it develop and progress, give it a voice, let us hear it boom out to all and sundry. A tribe is formed, a movement of followers, believers, fans, admirers.

Wow, how a humble idea seed consisting of opinions, views, thoughts, feelings and attitudes, can grow into an incredible vast forest of promise and possibility!

Often in life, those forests are cut down and reappear as hurdles, obstacles and fences. Challenges that we come across and take on and address on a daily basis.

✗ *Ideas are formed in the mind but triumph in the heart.*

Under Starters Orders

At the beginning of this book we spoke about aspiring to be a starter. We have travelled onwards together, we've climbed mountains, continually progressing to a variety of landmarks, destinations or key markers on our journey.

We have looked to act differently, to endure and to share our story. We now know we have the ability to teach the world to sing, to create genius and be mathematicians. We can stand for something, be original, remarkable, innovative and inspiring.

Often people refer to being blinkered as a negative thing, but perhaps it is an action to be applauded. A horse is often blinkered to keep it focused, to stop it from being distracted, potentially upset by what is going on around it. I believe that so it is with us as individuals – we can often be led astray by the actions of others, kept busy with side projects that distract us from having or setting long term goals, aims or ambitions.

Blinkers could help us immensely…… try it! Remember I talk fast so….

Switch off your iPod, come away from the web, leave behind your social media site for an hour or two. Do something different, brighten someone's day, relax and appreciate life. Turn off the TV, put down your newspaper and forget going out for the evening! Pick up and attach your blinkers –

Focus on setting, working toward and achieving. Believe in yourself, your skills and talents, identify them. Reflect on your life, share your stories and your experiences in a positive, constructive and uplifting way.

Volunteer, serve, make a difference in your community.

Small, daily or weekly actions that with the help of others will collectively enable you to leave behind a considerable and worthwhile legacy.

Blinkers on – Clear the hurdles – Complete the race – Be victorious – and I'll greet you at the finish line!

VICTUS

VICTUS CONSULTANCY

When was the last time you did something for the first time?

Employ our services to partner up on your projects now.

For more information on how we can help you increase your profitability and grow your business, contact Andrew.

✉ andrew@victusconsultancy.co.uk

☎ 07732 454639

💻 www.victusconsultancy.co.uk

www.ingramcontent.com/pod-product-compliance
Lightning Source LLC
Chambersburg PA
CBHW072227170526
45158CB00002BA/785